Sex, Lies, and Postage Stamps

by

Nathan La-monta James

Dorrance Publishing Co
585 Alpha Drive
Pittsburgh, PA 15238
Visit our website at *www.dorrancebookstore.com*

ISBN: 979-8-88729-337-0
eISBN: 979-8-88729-837-5

This is dedicated to Miss Diane, who simply told me very spiritually that one should never bite the hand that feeds one.... And you were so right completely.

Table of Contents

1.) Ordered by Captain to join Post Office 1
2.) Permanent Part-Time Postal Employee 3
3.) No School for Little Fools 5
4.) Permanent Slave Employee for Good Workers Only! .9
5.) S.E.X. ([3 2 1]) 11
6.) Sex Story One (Mechanic's Little Helper) 13
7.) Sex Story Two (I thwt I saw a Puddy Cat) 15
8.) Postal Story One (40 to 1) 17
9.) Postal Story Two (Is that a Joke?) 19
10.) Sex Story Three (The Night Man) 21
11.) Sex Story Four (One Glance, One Hit) 23
12.) Postal Story Three (Work till you freeze Old Lady) .25
13.) Postal Story Four (Post Office Peasants!) 27
14.) Shout Out One (Inexpensive Spirituality) 31
15.) Shout Out Two (The Missing One Million) 33
16.) Sex Story Five (The Postal Conductor) 35
17.) Sex Story Six (One Slice of Postal Dice) 39
18.) Postal Story Five (A Sad Day in Postal History) 43
19.) Shout Out Three (Climb Mountains) 45
20.) Postal Story Six (Friend No More!) 49
21.) Sex Story Seven (A Secret Crush and a Stamp) 53
22.) Sex Lies and Postage Stamps (The end) 59

Chapter One

I was ordered by a captain in the army to go and seek out a job at the post office. Since he was of a higher rank than me, I did what he wanted me to do. It was a spiritual blessing I'll never forget, even though I have forgotten his name. He had a program that he wanted all of us to transition into civilian life and get a job at the post office because congress and the government would back us up forever for our service and commitment to the United States of America and he was right. Thank you, sir. You know who you are.

Thank you so very much,

Staff Sergeant Nathan La-monta James.

Chapter Two

I started my postal career as a mail handler, but that only lasted five months because I did not like not having two days off to recover from the heavy work of lifting and moving the mail. So I took a job at a lower rank to clean the post office which made me a regular employee on the first day of service and I had two days off. thank you, Lord. Thank you, Jesus.

I must admit to you that I was embarrassed on my first day of work as a custodian because I had to clean up around the bundle sorter machine which is the same machine that I used to dump mail on. The people remembered me, and they looked down on me for going to a lower rank and having what they thought was a lower job than theirs. So I had to deal with it for about nine months. But what they didn't know is that I was taking tests and doing interviews to become a mechanic helper level five and I got the new job. You wouldn't believe that my first day of work was to work on and fix the bundle sorter machine. Now ain't that a kick in the head? People remembered me and they got confused, but they also got excited, and they said to me, "Wait a minute, wait a minute, aren't you the same guy that was dumping mail here and then you were cleaning the floor here and now you're fixing the machine here?" and I had to be humble. I was becoming spiritual, and I said, "Yes, I'm the same guy" and they said, "We want to be like you."

Chapter Three

As a maintenance mechanic level five, I was told that I could not go to school for training unless I was a level seven mail processing equipment mechanic because those seats in school were rare, special, and were not to be wasted on level five mechanics. But again, spiritually, an opportunity for me to go to school came along. I should explain that to you it was a level seven mechanic who was a tall Hercules-type gentleman and he couldn't find a safe place to leave his dog while he went to school, so he told management that he wasn't going to school. They got into a big argument but management was afraid of this guy and this guy was steadfast. He meant what he said, so now there was a seat open in school and management turned and looked down the hall and saw me.

They said, "James, you're going to school" because they didn't want to waste the seat and within three days, I was sitting in school in Norman, Oklahoma for training at the postal training facility. It was awesome and also very hard. My brain felt like it was going to explode because what I didn't know was, they had crammed information designed for a year's training into weeks, five weeks, six weeks, and examinations were timed. You had to have a seventy percent in order to pass the course. It was murder y'all. But I passed, and I returned to Washington DC with a certificate for my first class. Then, all of a sudden, another class opened up and I passed that one and another class opened up and I passed that one. I passed nine straight classes and guess what I was doing on my off time? I was taking other classes on the computer in my downtime at work and passing those also. All together, I passed 100 United States postal service training classes and then the union upgraded my rank from level five to level seven mechanic. but everyone else had an upgrade also, so I still had work to do. I still had to take examinations and interviews. Finally, I passed and received the job as a level nine mail processing equipment mechanic and to keep this story short, I didn't like what I was doing because it was too much work for a worker and too much money for a non-worker. Those are my words and I'm sticking by them.

So I got a promotion to heating and air conditioning mechanic level nine. I didn't realize that fixing heating and air conditioning for the post office was quite dangerous, climbing up ladders in 100-degree heat, everybody sweating, waiting for you to fix it. Oh baby, this thing was something else. But I was humbly dealing with it until we got brand new vehicles in the field maintenance department. I never got a brand-new vehicle. I was the only one driving an old beat-up vehicle. The new vehicles had a lot of space, a lot of comfort, so I changed back to mail processing equipment mechanic, and I changed tours from day to night to evening. I hadn't been to school in a long time, and I started asking if I could go to school again.

They tried to trick me at that point because I was still taking the examinations and interviews. I was on the promotion list for level ten and level eleven, so they tried to trick me by saying,

“Were going to promote you to level ten, but it is mandatory that you have to go to school two times within one year. Please don’t take this promotion if you don’t want to go to school now.”

What was I to do? Come on y’all, all I want to do is go to school so I took the promotion to level ten. I found out later that it was a lie. They wanted me to turn down the promotion so they could give it to their friend, a new guy who just came in the post office. I didn’t know anything about that at the time, but when I took the promotion, they stuck me with the new guy who had been working on the machine that I had never seen and never been to school for. It made me look stupid and dumb and the guy every day was trying to pick a fight with me. Now why did they put me with this guy? They wanted me to fight this guy so that I could be demoted, and he could be promoted, but it didn’t work because I was senior. So I bidded to another tour and bidded out of the building. That was my only escape from bad management.

Chapter Four

As an electronic technician level ten and with all the training that I had received and achieved over the years, along with my seniority, placed me in a very precarious situation of being taken advantage of. What I mean is I had no excuse and no way out of completing any job that anyone who called himself management would order me to do. The union confirmed that along with management and safety.

Well, as anyone could tell you or maybe you already know, over a period of thirty years, doing a lot of work and covering a lot of people who are not ordered to do work, your body starts to break down if you don't take care of it. I did not take care of my body because of the frustration of my mind, and I had to do certain things that one would normally not do in order to keep my sanity. So in essence, writing this book is sort of like therapy to me and informative to you, I hope.

I turned down the interview for electronic technician level eleven, but I did put in my application for over thirty maintenance supervisor jobs. Management never gave me an interview because they never wanted me to leave the floor and they never wanted me to hit the clock without a toolbox until the day I die. So many of my friends have worked themselves to death because of the amount of money that you can make in just two weeks doing overtime, family time, holiday time. Out of schedule pay working seven days a week, you can literally work yourself to death for the money. That has never been my problem ever because I've always told management that I'm rich... b****. They never understood that that meant that I was spiritually rich among all of God's children on the planet and throughout the galaxy and the universe.

Now let's move on to another part of this title, sex.

Chapter Five

S.E.X. is the title to a song I wrote many years ago a rap song that explains my emotional feelings about sex and what one had to go through to get at it and the repercussions one has to go through, after it's all said and done.

At the very end of the song, I wrote something that goes a little like this, with strong convictions and a tantalizing message for the young and for the old.

S is situations that emotions control.

E is ecstasy by remote control.

X is the extra that can't be denied

If you do it wrong, somebody dies!

I plan to remix all my songs, 300 of them, and release them to the public on my own record label after I retire from the post office and I find good people to work with.

Chapter Five

Chapter Six

(Sex Story One)

I was fixing a mailbox in northeast Washington DC. A pretty young lady came up to me smiling, showing me affection, and asked me if I had a cigarette that she could have.

I decided to see just how far this meeting could go so I said to her, "Here is enough money to buy a pack of cigarettes. You go get the cigarettes, bring them back and we'll share them."

I did this to see if she would take the money and go away or would she return with the cigarettes because I wanted to go further with this intriguing first meeting that we were having.

She came back with the cigarettes and as I was working, she asked me all kinds of personal, direct, and very poignant questions about us getting together and hooking up. She was so confident with what she was saying and what she was doing. I was not used to that type of confidence in a female before.

I've heard stories about these types of meetings before from other people, but now it seems like it was happening to me. I had to find out if it was going to turn out to be something of a memory or just a waste of time, energy, effort, and wishful thinking.

So, I gave in to her demands just to see how far she would allow me to go.

She said, "When you're done, drive around through the alley and I'll show you where we can go and finish our business and be alone to have some real fun together."

I finished what I was doing, and I drove around to the alley and there she was. She directed me to come inside of an empty shelter. Once inside, it just seemed like we had planned this. We were caught up in the moment and it just seemed like a date, if you ask me. We just hit it off and we were just making a memory between two people in time that day...

Once it was over, I felt sad inside because I had questions and I wanted answers. I wanted to see her again to be around her again, but I knew that it could not be.

So I just asked her straight out, "Why are you doing this?" and her answer was a shocker to my system she said, "Why would I stop doing something that's fun?"

I guess I just had to know. I was blown away because she was so pretty, and she had so much potential. What we were doing was the opposite of fun. It was very dangerous and irresponsible and a nude rebellion against decency.

Her name was Moe-shawn and I really liked her name. It played a very vital role in the actions that followed.

Chapter Seven

(Sex Story Two)

I was driving down the street in northwest DC, this fine beautiful uneventful day on the job. I looked to the right, just being observant, and I saw a Caucasian pretty young lady sitting on the porch with her legs wide open and I could see her panties so... I didn't think that the post office would mind if I went around the block and came down the street one more time just to make sure that my eyes and my mind were on the same page.

As I came down the street again, the young lady signaled me to pull over and stop and come and see her. So myself being a very helpful postal employee, I figured she had some questions about her mailbox that she needed answers for. So I pulled over and I'm no dummy, I took a baby sledgehammer and the longest screwdriver that I had in my tool kit, and I went up to the yard where she was at.

She said, "Come on in, come on in. Let's talk a while."

I went inside and this was a relaxed atmosphere with people minding their own business and not caring about what was going on around them. So I went to the back bedroom with her.

She said, "Do you have any money? We can have sex."

I just happened to have some money and she had a condom. We proceeded to have an uninterrupted memory and a small business transaction. I did take a look at the mailbox also while I was there.

As I was leaving, she said, "Can you give me a ride down the street?"

And then I said, "I'm going straight down the street but I'm not making any turns. So when we get to the last stop sign before the bridge, I'm going straight across the bridge and I'm not bending on that."

She said, "It's okay. I just want to go straight down the street, and I'll be fine"

I was like, "Okay, let's go."

As we started driving straight down the street, the strangest thing in the world happened. There was a car that was on my right side that kept inching forward, trying to get in the lane that I was in. So I stopped the truck I was driving to allow the car to go in front of me. But what was really happening is that there was a lady in that car who must have been an employee of the post office a long time ago, because she wrote down my tag number and then she drove away.

I said, "Oh my God, she's going to report me to the post office."

So I let the young lady out down the street and my nerves were gone for a couple of weeks. But I'm a man within my flesh, so whatever the complaint that comes to me, I just have to deal with it. But after a couple of weeks of no one alerting me to a complaint or write up, I remembered that she made a mistake also. What I mean is she wrote down the license plate number to the truck I was driving, but that license plate was ten to twelve years old. It had been used on many vehicles in that period of time. The number she should have written down was on the side of the truck, not the license plate number. So she messed up and I truly believe she used to be a postal employee who did more talking than researching the situation or problem!

Chapter Eight

(Postal Story One)

My supervisor gave me a work order to fix one ceiling light over this employee's workstation in the post office box section. Once I was finished with that work order and about to pack up my tools and leave, I noticed five employees surrounding me and asking me if I could fix the rest of the lights that were off and broken in that section. There were about forty lights that needed to be fixed and, without authorization, I fixed them all. But the interesting fact of the matter is that when I was done, the employees told me that they were trying to get those lights fixed for two years. That hurt me to my heart, and I can't explain that to you with a sensible answer.

Chapter Nine

(Postal Story Two)

I had just finished unjamming the sack sorter conveyor belts on the computer screen and all the mail sacks we're moving along fantastically. As I eased the chair back to stand up, the chair was defective and threw me backwards. I hit my neck on the corner of the case on the wall and I was hurt and in extreme pain, so I reported it to the supervisor over the radio.

The supervisor came to the control room, and he said to me, "Are you playing a game? You're not really hurt."

I said, "Yes sir, I'm hurt. I need to go to the hospital."

He said, "Well, if you are hurt then you fill out the accident forms."

As I reached into the accident folder and started filling out the accident forms, that's when he said, "Well, I guess you are hurt. Let me go get the postal truck so I can take you to the hospital now."

It was very shocking to me that he thought I was playing a joke, but we went to the hospital, I received treatment, and I was off from work for two weeks.

But the interesting thing here was that when I returned to work a few days after, I received a call from a safety lady employee and she said,

"Mr. James, you've had two accidents. If you have one more accident on the clock, you will be fired."

I said to her the first accident I had was almost two years ago and she said it doesn't matter, three accidents in your career and you are fired. This was shocking information to me and quite unbelievable.

Chapter Ten

(Sex Story Three)

I was the only one on the clock in my section at the end of the day. I was called the night man. If all of my work was completed, I would have about an hour and a half or close to two hours downtime before I went home, so what I would do is watch a DVD movie in the boss's office just to kill some time. But this particular day, I stopped at the liquor store and bought a couple of wine coolers and some spicy hot pork skins.

A young Oriental woman was standing outside the liquor store and asked me if I had some money I could give her.

I said, "Sure I have a couple of dollars I can spare."

She said, "Thanks but could we possibly have a small business arrangement for some extra money?"

I said, "Sure, but you have to take a ride with me around the corner into a little shelter that I have the keys to."

She said okay and we drove around to the office, which is detached from the main post office, and we had a small, interesting form of sex in the secretary's office. After we were done, I took her downstairs, and I looked out the door and smoked a cigarette, made sure there was no traffic and no one around.

I let her out the door and said, "Thanks, see you later."

You know time flies when you're having fun.

Chapter Ten

Chapter Eleven

(Sex Story Four)

I bumped into a young lady that I knew from way back. I had a crush on her since the first time I saw her and, surprisingly enough, it was her first day working at the post office. After we greeted each other, she was so angry and upset. I asked her if she wanted a ride home and she said, "yeah". So we both got off about the same time and I drove her home.

As we sat outside of her house in the car, she said, "That was my first day working in the post office and my last day. No one talks to me like I'm a child. I quit."

I said, "Wow, are you serious?"

She said, "Yeah, that's right. I'm not going back there ever again," and she meant what she was saying. Then she looked me right in my face and asked me if we ever had sex before.

I said, "No, I would definitely remember."

She said, "Well, come on in. Tonight is your special night."

Thank you post office for losing an employee and making me a sexual memory. Her name is Teresa and we never hooked up again.

Chapter Twelve

(Postal Story Three)

I was sent from the main building to a smaller post office to fix a hand dryer in the ladies' room and a small space heater in one of the offices. When I pulled up at the back dock and parked my truck, I grabbed two small tool bags and went inside the double doors leading from the dock to the inside of the post office. There was an older lady employee bundled up real tight and working on this freezing dock by herself with no heat.

So, I said to her, "Hey young lady, why are you working out here without any heat?"

She pointed up in the ceiling and said, "That heater up there has been broke for two winters."

So I looked at her and I said, "I got you."

So, without authorization, I came back the next day and I fixed the heater. It was warm and feeling good out there on that dock, so I went inside to report it to the pretty, lovely, young supervisor woman. I told her that when that young lady comes back who works out on the dock, let her know that the heat is working and, you're not going to believe this, that supervisor lady said, "What? She don't need no damn heat," and she turned the heater off and walked away from me.

Now that was horrible. It hurt my heart, but I couldn't do anything about it because I wasn't even authorized to fix it. So I just sucked it up. Another lesson learned about postage stamps and me.

Chapter Twelve

Chapter Thirteen

(Postal Story Four)

There is a small post office in southwest Washington DC across the street from the DMV office. This little post office was totally destroyed, and it looked as if it was contaminated. In the bathrooms and the break room and even in the men's and women's locker rooms , and it even had thirty lights out.

Chapter Thirteen

(Postal Story Four continued)

I was very sad that day to be a part of this organization and to see postal employees having to endure this type of degradation. So, I went to work, day after day, unauthorized and I brought the standards of the men's and women's bathrooms up, the men's and women's locker rooms up, the main break room down in the basement, and I even fixed those thirty lights on the workroom floor that were out for a couple of years. I even went as far as to fix the wall protection sleeves and wood sheets and while I was there, I fixed a couple of doors to a couple of offices. I fixed at least twelve cash drawers that needed new locks because people who work those cash drawers had left employment years ago. I even fixed some post office boxes that needed new locks in the main lobby to generate money for the post office.

Of course when management caught up with me and found out what I was doing, this one manager accused me of stealing overtime on the post office clock. That was a bad day that we both had in the office. I closed his door and asked him if he really wanted to talk about this or was he going to stop calling me a thief. He asked me to open his door back up and to get off his clock and never let it happen again because I didn't have paperwork that authorized me to do what I did. He didn't believe that I did it anyway. Man, sometimes it hurts to try to help an organization that can't tell the difference between a worker and a liar.

Chapter Thirteen

Chapter Fourteen

(Shout Out One)

I would like to take the time to let everyone know that I wrote a really good book for the world, and it was published by Dorrance Publishing. I believe in my heart that the first book I wrote could really change a lot of people's lives. If you ever wanted to give someone a special gift for a birthday, a holiday gift, or a special gift for a friend, the book I wrote is the one. Especially for those with no hope left inside and too much pride to ask for help on the outside of them.

(*The 66 Books of Nathan Spiritual Understandings*)

Chapter Fifteen

(Shout Out Two)

The post office has paid me benefits equaling to or a little more than $2 million in a thirty-year career and believe me y'all, I have earned my pay. Some employees have told me over the years that we should have received more according to the public standards, so that means I'm missing a million dollars somewhere. But I could not have ever thought when I was a child growing up that I would have touched that much money in my life. I don't care about the missing million dollars. I just want to thank the post office for the $2 million dollars. I have accomplished a couple of things and I've helped the homeless with way more than thirty-four to forty-seven percent of that $2 million dollars and with the books I've written. So thank you for the money and you're welcome for the work. We made a good pair; good enough to help those who needed help and myself.

Chapter Sixteen

(Sex Story Five)

I am no longer married so I can tell this story now.

I have been to the postal training academy in Norman Oklahoma eleven times and the post office reimbursed me for every one of those experiences. But being who I am, I was a little different from the other employees because I took the Amtrak train for three days going to the facility and three days coming back home. That was six days of very interesting scenery and memories, delicious food, drink, and sleeping compartment cars, along with a personal attendant and free coffee, juice, and wine at all times. Also, some of the most fantastic conversations with people from all around the world, all different types. It was the most amazing, fun, and relaxing experience that I have ever had on vacation.

I remember this dark chocolate, very jovial young lady who was getting on the train with assistance from the employees.

She hollered out, "There are no seats up here."

That's when I hollered out, "There's a seat right here beside me and compartments for your bags if you'd like to sit here."

She said, "Oh yes, I didn't see that."

So we got her tucked in and she didn't realize that I was just sitting there for company. I had a compartment in the back, I just wanted to come up and sit amongst the common folks for a while before dinner. She was in luck because they were taking orders for dinner, and I asked her to join me because the people with the sleeping compartments have first choice for dinner reservations. So I made reservations for two for dinner and we went to the observation deck. We started to have nice cool drinks, whatever she wanted. We were talking, and she was explaining to me that she was receiving help trying to get back home to Dallas, Texas, but her ticket was about to run out in the next few stops, and she had no money to complete her training reservations. So I picked up my phone. I asked for her ticket. I called the Amtrak counter, and I had her ticket extended all the way to Dallas, Texas, I paid for it, and that was that. She was so happy.

Her story was a sad one. The guy she was traveling with asked her to go with him on a business trip just to keep him company on the long drive. But once he got her away from Dallas, Texas, he started making demands for sex and other things. When she got a chance, she just grabbed her things and left and went to a shelter. The shelter put her up and got her a ticket. They took up a collection and they did a great job. She ended up meeting me, so we had dinner. We had snacks and we talked all night long.

We arrived in Chicago and there was a five-hour layover, so I rented a motel, and we got drunk. We took showers, and we had fun. She really liked me because I wasn't forcing myself on her and I made her laugh and I laughed with her. So now the train was about to pull out from Chicago, and she took a nap, but I did not dare go to sleep. I didn't want to miss the train. I still had a responsibility to show up at postal school in Norman, Oklahoma.

So we got back on the train and that's when she discovered I had a sleeping compartment. We went to my sleeping compartment with some more drinks and snacks, and we had a good time all night until we were awoakened by the attendant, who asked us if we wanted breakfast or not. Of course we said, "Yes, breakfast would be awesome right now." We had a delicious breakfast with scenery and conversation. We exchanged telephone numbers and addresses because she definitely wanted to see me again while I had my four weeks stay in Norman, Oklahoma, which was not far away from her. So we reached Texas and she had to leave me in order to catch another train to Dallas and I had to leave that train in order to catch a quick two-hour train to Norman, Oklahoma.

Once that first weekend came, I called her, and we made arrangements for a date. I rented a car and went down to Dallas, Texas and picked her up. She wanted me to meet some of her friends and family but I told her that was not a good idea. This weekend let's just have fun and we'll try that the next weekend. That was three of the best weekends of my life, but I did not see her on that last weekend because I was married, and I started having really strong feelings for her. So I gave her as much money as I could give her on a post office paycheck, and I deleted her number from my phone for good.

Her name was Charmaine, and she was great to me.

Chapter Seventeen

(Sex Story Six)

Her name was Miss Janice, and she was a classy older woman. We were in maintenance class together in Norman, Oklahoma. I didn't really notice her at first, but she smoked cigarettes the same as I, so I got to know a little bit about her and her character. The one thing that stood out very clearly was that she wore a lot of jewelry, beautiful jewelry, real jewelry. Other than that, she was just very confident, very jovial, happy, and she was always on the phone directing her life. She was dealing with her ex-husband and his alimony payments. She was dealing with her granddaughter. Deadbeat Daddy didn't want to pay up and her daughter's situation. She was dealing with her ex-husband's family members trying to take things out of her house from the divorce. Like I said before, I just noticed that about her.

But one Friday evening I was at the River wind casino, and she saw me there and recognized me from class. She asked me if I liked the casino. I told her that I didn't have a car. The shuttle bus brought me to this casino and it was okay for what I was trying to do.

So she said, "Come on with me and I'll take you to Texas to a casino that I like."

So we hopped in her car, and we started driving for about two hours and we got to the casino that she liked. Sorry, I can't tell you the name of it. She told me where she would be and she said if I was ready to leave, come and find her or have her paged. So I had a pretty good time and then she came upon me, I was playing this one machine and I was down to my last $2 in the machine. I wasn't broke, but she thought that that was all the money I had. She gave me $100 and said, "Have fun," and she walked away. So I decided to get something to eat and just sit and watch the other people gambling.

Well, she came up to find me and saw that I was eating, and she said, "Are you ready to go home yet?"

I said, "Anytime you are."

She said, "Well, I'm a winner and I'm ready to leave."

I said, "So am I."

So we got in the car and we started to drive back to the post office campus. But an interesting thing was happening. As she was driving she started to fall asleep at the wheel and I cautioned her, and I woke her up. She kept doing it.

I said to her, "I have a driver's license, I can drive the rest of the way."

She said, "I never let anyone drive my car."

I said, "Well, I'm not going to risk my life by you being so sleepy. Why don't you stop at a gas station so we can get some coffee and some snacks? We'll just stop as many times as we have to until we get back to campus."

She said, "I have a better idea, let's stop at a motel."

I said, "That works for me," because at this point my life was on the line.

So when we got into the motel, she said she needed a shower.

I said, "It's okay, I'll just sit outside in the car and listen to some music until you're done and then I'll come in and sleep on the floor."

So after a while of listening to music, I came back inside, and she was in bed.

She said, "It's your turn to take a shower."

So when I finished my shower I came out and she said, "Get in the bed and cuddle with me. I like to celebrate when I'm a winner at the casino."

So I got in the bed, and she was completely nude. We made love, and it was great. We fell off to sleep and when we woke up in the morning, it was about 10:00 a.m.

She said, "Check out time is at 12:00. Do you have any energy left?"

I said, "Yes ma'am, I sure do," and we made love again.

She said, "We can't tell anyone about what we've done."

I said, "It works for me."

Thanks to the casino for making us both winners.

Chapter Eighteen

(Postal Story Five)

I finally lost control with management after twenty-six years, but I was saved by an employee who didn't like me and wanted my career to somehow be bad so that he could profit from my losses. That had to be something spiritual. Here's what happened that amazing and sad day.

Management called me on my telephone on my day off, one day before I had to travel to Norman, Oklahoma for training in school, and told me that my travel plans had not been taken care of by them. If I wanted to leave tomorrow, I had to come to work and take care of my travel plans myself with my own money. I went to the post office on my day off. I rode the subway down to the train station and I took care of all my travel plans with my money. Everything was set to go, all I had to do was go back to the post office and give the management a copy of the paperwork so that they could have it on file in case something happened to me on my way to postal training school. Once I had accomplished that, I thought since I was at the post office, I might speak to my friend over the radio and tell him to call me sometime within the next weeks. So I called out his name on the radio and he did not answer, but one of the supervisors came over the radio and told me that my friend was not at work today, he was on his off day. I said, "Okay and that was that, so I thought.

But then that same supervisor said over the radio loud and clear, “Mr. James, what are you doing with a post office radio in your hand? You are not supposed to be in my building today.”

Well, my good people, I lost control of everything, and I tried to grab that radio from Mr. Cruz, the employee who had let me use his radio. I wanted to fight and hurt and do something physical to that supervisor, but Mr. Cruz would not give me the radio back. He put his finger up in front of my face and wiggled it from left to right as if to say, “No, no, no.” In that short period of time, I caught my composure, put my two hands together as if I was praying, I bowed to Mr. Cruz, and backed away. I turned and I walked away and left the building,

If Mr. Cruz had given me that radio, I know my job would have been lost in the next few minutes and I wasn’t going to stop. I just had enough of degradation, intimidation, and unprofessionalism, and I really wanted to make it equal. I planned to do that and I wasn’t going to stop no matter what. But I was saved.

And this is one of the deciding factors of why I must retire from the post office because bad professionalism gets to me after a long period of time, day after day, week after week, month after month, year after year. I just have to be rid of it altogether.

Chapter Nineteen

(Shout Out Three)

This is a positive rap song that I had the honor of performing at the black history celebration every year at the post office. A positive rap song I wrote called, "Climb Mountains". Here are the lyrics to this song that I wrote forty years ago. I hope you like it. If anyone would like to copyright this song and sing it to the world, I would never ever try to sue you, for that it would be a blessing on top of a blessing. You can use this book as proof that I will not sue you. Copyright the song and perform it to the world. I'm getting a little old now and I would like for this song to carry on!

Well, to be a mountain climber here's what you do
You start off by simply going to school
And then you study super hard and answer some questions
After passing the test, you make some suggestions
Now you're graduating, the world is just waiting
You formulate your plans 'cuz your regulating
Never seek and search with two empty hands
Stand tall and proud and say here's my game plan.

(Chorus)
Climb mountains until you reach the top
Don't stop, don't stop, don't ever stop.

The first step you take is getting rid of the hate
Let's go to work, clean the dirt that people make
Step two is to do things that need to be done
You can't find nothing to do, you go back to step one
The third step on the mountain is to keep yourself happy
I'll do the rapping, you do the clapping
Step four is the door 'cuz it's hardcore
No turning back now 'cuz it's time to score.

(Chorus)
Climb mountains until you reach the top
Don't stop, don't stop, don't ever stop.

Now step five is live, you have way no jive
And the feelings that you feel means you're going to survive.
Step six is full of tricks like a dog with ticks
But when you practice with the clocks, you move with the clicks.
Step seven is heaven and now you go bragging
Funky fresh dress and ice-cold ragging
Step eight is great, so participate
'Cuz mountain climbers catching on it and incredible rate.

(Chorus)
Climb mountains until you reach the top
Don't stop, don't stop, don't ever stop.

Now step nine is mine so let me take my time

And cold put it ending on this funky rhyme
'Cuz the crew that's the best is yo-jam is fresh
And the leader that's me, cold beat Master free.
Jazziano is my friend till death do us in
I hope you understand it 'cuz that's step ten
I'm climbing out of here and I have no fear
You want education then you'll come right here

And climb mountains until you reach the top
And don't stop, don't stop, don't ever stop.
You climb mountains until you reach the top and don't stop, huh!

Now I've been waiting for this date
I've been waiting to state
My case to you, I'll show you I'm not fake
And motivate you all to show do and prove
And let him know outside that we're in the groove
I'm not about throwing fists, education don't miss
And if you have common sense, you can get with this.
Because the stronger you are
The more mountains you move
And the longer you live
That means you will not lose

So climb mountains until you reach the top
And don't stop, don't stop, don't ever stop.
Climb mountains until you reach the top and don't stop, huh!

Chapter Twenty

(Postal Story Six)

This is about a postal friend no more.

My friend Andre called me and asked me to come over to his house for a very special gift. We had only known each other for about four years in the post office, so when I went over to his house, he started to tell me a story and the story went something like this.

He had made a take-home paycheck of $3,000 in two weeks working at the post office, so he went to the liquor store to cash his $3,000 check. There was a very pretty young lady at the cashier window, and he started flirting with her right away. She loved it and she was flirting back. They were completing their transaction but at the end of the transaction, she gave him the $3,000 and she gave him the check back.

He said to her "I'm not going to wait a long time for you to call me."

She said, "I'm going to call you soon."

He said, "Okay, bye."

Then he walked down the street to another liquor store and re-cashed the $3,000 check. He went to the Western Union, and he sent his mother about $1,200 and then he bought a brand-new computer, some movies, a bunch of liquor, beer, and reefer. Then he called me and told me to come over for a very special gift.

Now after he told me that story, I was sitting there and I said to him, "Why in the world did you do that? You probably got that young lady fired from her job because there is no way you can explain $3,000 missing. Even if she gets to keep her job, she's going to have to pay that $3,000 back. Why did you do that?"

He said, "That was her stupid mistake, not mine."

I said, "Yeah, but there's a time and place for everything, man. That was not the time or the place to keep that check and walk down the street and re-cash it. That was just not a good solid move. Now that you told me, you can still go back to that liquor store and give that young lady that $3,000 back."

He said, "No way, she messed up, that was her fault. I'm looking at it like a blessing."

I said, "Well my friend, we cannot be friends ever again."

I hadn't spoken to him for seventeen straight years until one day I was waiting for a call from Texas and the phone rang. It had a Texas area code. I answered it and it was Andre.

He said, "How are you doing?"

I said, "Fine."

He said, "Well, I'm living in El Paso, Texas now and I have re-married a new wife. I took a medical retirement from the post office and I'm here raising kids with my new wife. If you're ever in El Paso, Texas or close by, call me and come by and meet the wife."

I said, "Okay," to him just to be nice. But I really said okay because the postal training school is in Norman, Oklahoma which is not far from El Paso, Texas and I just figured that if I ever go to school and training at the post office campus, I would rent a car, drive down, say "hi" to him to meet his new wife, say "hi" to the kids, and turn around and go back to the campus. It's been twenty-five years now and I don't think that I'll ever check in with this man again because he showed me his true character in a situation in which he could have caused no harm but did anyway. I don't want to be friends with postal people like that ever again in my life.

Chapter Twenty-One

(Sex Story Seven)

One day I was laying on the floor fixing post office box locks at the old postal museum and I heard a young lady call out my name.

"Nathan, is that you?"

I said, "Yes, it is."

She said, "I have someone outside waiting for me but I'm going to give you my phone number. Call me and I'll cook you dinner."

When I looked back and she came to give me her number, it was Annabelle Carter, the young lady I had a crush on so hard when I was small before I left home. The last time I saw her was in the basement of her mother's house and here's what happened.

I took three buses in order to get over to her house to see her and they invited me to dinner.

After dinner, Annabelle said, "It's too late for Nathan to catch the bus back to Southeast. He's going to sleep with me in the basement."

I was embarrassed because her mother and her grandmother heard it, but no one said anything. So after everyone went upstairs, Annabelle and I went into the basement. She freshened up and got in bed. I just took off my shoes and laid on the bed. She fell off to sleep pretty quickly, but I stayed up all night, just admiring her, on my elbow. It was the greatest night I ever spent, watching this beautiful young lady that I wanted for my wife.

Then she woke up and she said, "Have you been staring at me all night?"

I said, "Yes ma'am, I sure have."

The family had cooked breakfast and said, "Y'all come up to breakfast."

I went up, ate breakfast and I left and went home. That was the last time I saw her until she gave me her number and told me to call her, and she would cook me dinner. So I told my wife that after work Saturday I was going to watch football over my friend's house for the rest of the evening and I probably would spend the night over his house. She said, "okay," so the next day I called in for work and about 1:00 I called Annabelle and asked her if it was okay for me to come to dinner. She said, "yes."

She gave me her address and I went over there. She told me where to park and gave me a parking plaque so that they wouldn't tow away my vehicle. When I came into her apartment, she grabbed my face with her hands and just looked at me and hugged me so tightly. It was the greatest hug I ever had.

Then she asked me, "What do you want me to cook you for dinner?"

I said, "A bowl of cereal," and we laughed so hard. I said, "A bowl of oatmeal and boiled eggs," and we laughed. I mean we laughed so hard.

Then I said, "You know what? Could you cook me a bowl of noodles and a couple of boiled eggs?"

She said, "Why do you want me to cook that?"

I said, "Because the last time I saw you, I went to Korea and every time I would think about you, I would have a bowl of noodles and a couple of boiled eggs and that's what I want."

She said, "Okay sit on the couch I'll bring you some wine and I'll cook you some noodles 'cuz I got a lot to tell you. I got a lot to say to you."

So I sit on the couch. She brought me wine. She cooked my noodles and then she came and sat on the couch with her wine.

She said, "I know you had a crush on me, but at the time I was a fast girl because I was trying to be the most popular girl. I was trying to meet an older man so I could move in with him and move out of my mother's house. I didn't hate being in my mother's house, but I really wanted to get out of my mother's house. I met a guy who was selling drugs. I moved in with him and I was helping him sell drugs. I kind of got hooked on the drugs and I didn't go back to school. I didn't want to do anything, and I got pregnant. I had the first child, and I still didn't want to do anything, you know, but smoke drugs. I got pregnant again and had a second child and I didn't want to do anything. I was just laying around gaining weight and so I turn my children over to my mother so that she could have custody. Then I saw you on television. When I saw you on television, I told my boyfriend and my girlfriends and the people I know that I knew you and I went to school with you and guess what? Every one of them called me a liar. It really hurt me because for the first time in my life I was telling everyone I knew the truth and not one of them believed me. I said, 'You know what? I'm going to change my life and I'm going to prove to them that I know you and I'm telling the truth.' So after that, I slowly started getting off drugs. I started going to the gym, losing weight, and I started going to night school. I was just going to get myself together and then I was going to find your phone number and call you. But then I saw you laying on the floor of the post office and I knew it was time. That's why I gave you my number and invited you to dinner."

I said, "Wow, that is an amazing story."

She said, "Yeah, so now I'm going to take pictures with you in my apartment and get your phone number. I'm going to prove to them all that I know you."

And we did just that.

After we were finished, she said, "Now I want to personally thank you for everything you have helped me accomplish. But in about four months, I'm going to marry a young man who has just become a new doctor. I met him in the gym, again thanks to you. So how deep is that crush you had on me?"

I said, "If I could have married you, I would have."

She said, "Well, tonight is your night if you want to make that crush and that dream come true. This is your one chance."

I said, "Absolutely," and I took a shower, and I sat on the couch.

She took a shower, and she came out the most beautiful sexy inspiring vision I have ever seen. We took our lovemaking from the couch to the bedroom and it was perfect.

When I woke up the next morning, she was leaning on her elbow and staring at me.

I said, "You're alright."

She said, "Yeah, I was just wondering if you had any more energy left."

I said, "yes," and we engaged in a second beautiful intimate love, and I have never seen her again.

Thanks post office. Thank you so much.

Chapter Twenty-Two

(Sex Lies and Postage Stamps The End)

It took me twenty-nine years to receive $1,500 a month retirement. But on December 1st 2022 I will receive $3,000 a month so I am out of here... (Postal out!)... I didn't get the postal police job because of a postal lie thank you God.

www.ingramcontent.com/pod-product-compliance
Lightning Source LLC
LaVergne TN
LVHW010504160826
845677LV00012B/2641

* 9 7 9 8 8 8 7 2 9 3 3 7 0 *